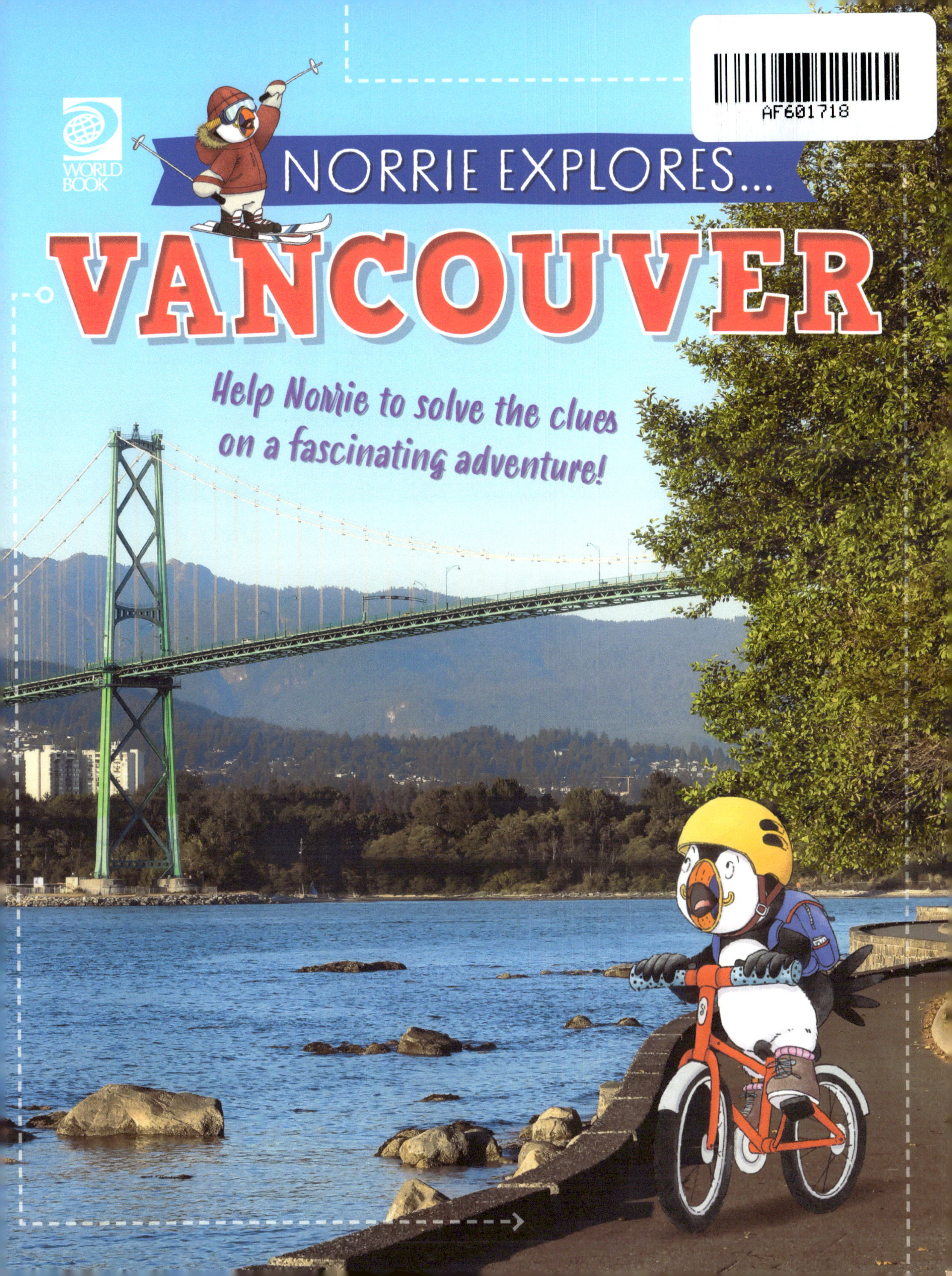
AF601718
WORLD BOOK
NORRIE EXPLORES...
VANCOUVER
Help Norrie to solve the clues on a fascinating adventure!

World Book, Inc.
180 North LaSalle Street
Suite 900
Chicago, Illinois 60601
USA

For information about other World Book publications, visit our website at www.worldbook.com or call 1-800-WORLDBK (967-5325). For information about sales to schools and libraries, call 1-800-975-3250 (United States), or 1-800-837-5365 (Canada).

Library of Congress Cataloging-in-Publication Data for this volume has been applied for.

Norrie Explores ...
ISBN: 978-0-7166-5303-5 (set, hc.)

Norrie Explores ... Vancouver
ISBN: 978-0-7166-5313-4 (hc.)
ISBN: 978-0-7166-5333-2 (pf.)

Also available as:
ISBN: 978-0-7166-5323-3 (e-book)

Staff

Executive Committee
President: Geoff Broderick
Vice President, Editorial: Tom Evans
Vice President, Finance: Donald D. Keller
Vice President, International: Eddy Kisman
Vice President, Technology: Jason Dole
Director, Human Resources: Bev Ecker

Editorial
Senior Editor/Indexer: Shawn Brennan
Editor/Researcher: Lynn Durbin
Content Creator: Jenna Neely
Curriculum Designer: Caroline Davidson
Project Coordinator: Kaile Kilner
Proofreader: Nathalie Strassheim

Graphics and Design
Senior Visual Communications Designer: Melanie Bender
Senior Media Editor: Rosalia Bledsoe

Acknowledgments

Writer: Izzi Howell
Illustrator: Lizzie Walkley

Developed with World Book by
White-Thomson Publishing LTD
www.wtpub.co.uk

Cover: Norrie artwork by Lizzie Walkley, Advocate Art; © edb3_16/iStock

4-5 © Karoline Cullen, Shutterstock
6-7 © All Canada Photos/Alamy Images; © Png Studio/Alamy Images
8-9 © Stefano Politi Markovina, Alamy Images; © IRC/Shutterstock; © Shaun Cunningham, Alamy Images
10-11 © Edgar Bullon, iStock; © SvetlanaSF/Shutterstock; © Sven Hofmann, Shutterstock
12-13 © Shawn.ccf/Alamy Images; © karamysh/Shutterstock
14-15 © Megapress/Alamy Images; © Harald Schmidt, Shutterstock; © Ronnie Chua, Shutterstock
16-17 © Ronnie Chua, Alamy Images; © Design Pics/Alamy Images
18-19 © Niels van Kampenhout, Alamy Images; © All Canada Photos/Alamy Images
20-21 © mj0007/iStock; © Michael Wheatley, Alamy Images
22-23 © John Mitchell, Alamy Images; © Klara Steffkova, Shutterstock; © Fang Xia Nuo, iStock
24-25 © Ron Niebrugge, Alamy Images; © Darryl Brooks, Shutterstock
26-27 © Jeff Whyte, Shutterstock; © ART Collection/Alamy Images; © bmf-foto.de/Shutterstock
28-29 © Sipa US/Alamy Images; © Norman Pogson, Alamy Images
30-31 © Shutterstock
32-33 © Ei Katsumata, Alamy Images; © Luca Pattini, Shutterstock; © Hugo Sena, Shutterstock
34-35 © Michael Euley, Alamy Images; © EB Adventure Photography/Shutterstock
36-37 © Jason Schnieder, Alamy Images; © Richard A McMillin, Shutterstock
38-39 © All Canada Photos/Alamy Images; © Alan Douglas, Alamy Images
40-41 © Ronnie Chua, Alamy Images; © Michael Wheatley, Alamy Images
42-43 © All Canada Photos/Alamy Images; © imageBROKER/Alamy Images; © Michael Wheatley, Alamy Images
46-47 © Shutterstock; Kallerna (licensed under CC BY-SA 4.0)
48-49 © Max Lindenthaler, Shutterstock; © I viewfinder/Shutterstock; © EB Adventure Photography/Shutterstock; © Michael Wheatley, Alamy Images; © Mayank Yadav, Shutterstock
50-51 © Shutterstock

Contents

Welcome to Vancouver!

Hi, I'm Norrie! I'm a puffin. I love to travel the world and explore different cities around the globe.

Today, I'm in Vancouver, one of the largest cities in Canada. Vancouver is found on the western edge of Canada, in the province of British Columbia. Have you ever visited Vancouver or Canada before?

The city of Vancouver was founded in 1865. Today, it is home to over 600,000 people. Vancouver is Canada's busiest port. It is known as Canada's "Gateway to the Pacific" because ships leave from here to trade with Japan and other nations of the Pacific Ocean rim. Vancouver's natural harbor never freezes – even though it is so far north. Ships can use it the year around.

I love taking photos of all the places that I visit! But this trip is a little different. I'm about to enter a big photography competition, and I need the perfect photo! I'm hoping I can take the photo somewhere here in Vancouver. I've put together a list of some different places and things I want to capture with my camera, so I don't forget anything. Will you help me explore the city and find the winning shot?

Museum of Anthropology

The Museum of Anthropology (the scientific study of human beings and human culture) is a great place to find out more about the people who first lived on this land thousands of years ago.

Many of their descendants still live here today. In Canada, they are called First Nations people or Indigenous people.

Many First Nations people fished for salmon and traveled local waters in their dugout canoes. They made these boats by hollowing out tree trunks. You can see some dugout canoes in the museum.

The museum's Great Hall is filled with large totem poles and sculptures.

In the Great Hall, look waaay up! The poles we see are First Nations totem poles, each one carved from a tall tree. Each pole is carved with different creatures, called totems. Each animal has a special meaning and helps to tell the family story, passed down from the elders to the young ones.

The museum also contains many objects from other countries around the world. You can see Chinese calligraphy, Japanese masks, jewelry from Ethiopia, Spanish lace, and weapons from the South Pacific Islands. Which exhibits would you like to see?

Outside the museum, there is a reconstructed village of the Haida First Nations people. The Haida traditionally lived on a group of islands to the north of Vancouver.

Stanley Park

Right next to the skyscrapers of downtown Vancouver are the towering forests of Stanley Park.

The parkland was set aside in the late 1800's, not long after the city was founded. Stanley Park is huge, bigger than 750 American football fields!

Have you ever hugged a huge tree before? Let's take a hike on the Lake Trail. Along these trails, you can find trees called western red cedars that reach 160 feet (50 meters) tall. These trees are three times taller than the totem poles we saw earlier.

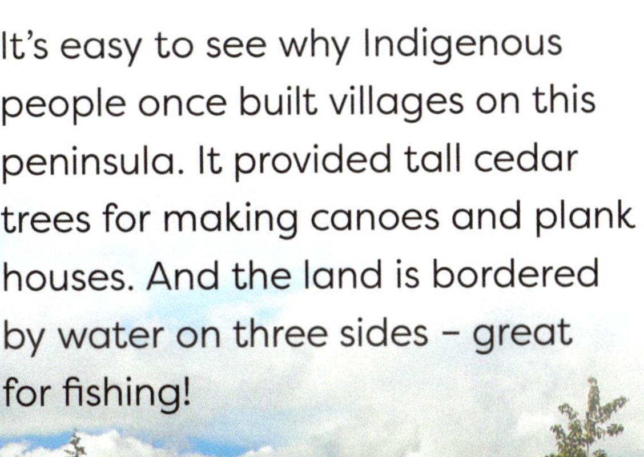

It's easy to see why Indigenous people once built villages on this peninsula. It provided tall cedar trees for making canoes and plank houses. And the land is bordered by water on three sides – great for fishing!

In this West Coast rain forest, even the ferns are taller than I am! Many animals, such as bats, beavers, squirrels, and raccoons, live among the trees and other plants in Stanley Park. If I'm very quiet, maybe I'll be able to get a photo of one of them!

Did I drop some of my banana?
No, this is a banana slug!

Banana slugs live on the forest floor. They stay in moist, damp areas so that they don't dry out.

If you see a large, messy pile of sticks in a treetop, it's probably a bald eagle nest. If you hear a sound like a squeaky wheel ... look up! It's probably a bald eagle!

There's so much more of Stanley Park to see. I'm going to rent a bike so I can feel the wind in my feathers! You can ride around the edge of Stanley Park on the sea wall. The sea wall is an embankment built to protect the land from ocean waves. The path goes all the way around the peninsula in a big loop. It takes about an hour. Well, maybe a little longer if you stop for ice cream! During springtime you'll smell the scent of roses and rhododendrons floating on the salty ocean air. In the fall, the green forest will change to bright oranges, reds, and yellows.

The path takes you beneath the Lions Gate Bridge. This suspension bridge carries automobile traffic across Burrard Inlet. It is named after the Lions, two mountain peaks north of Vancouver.

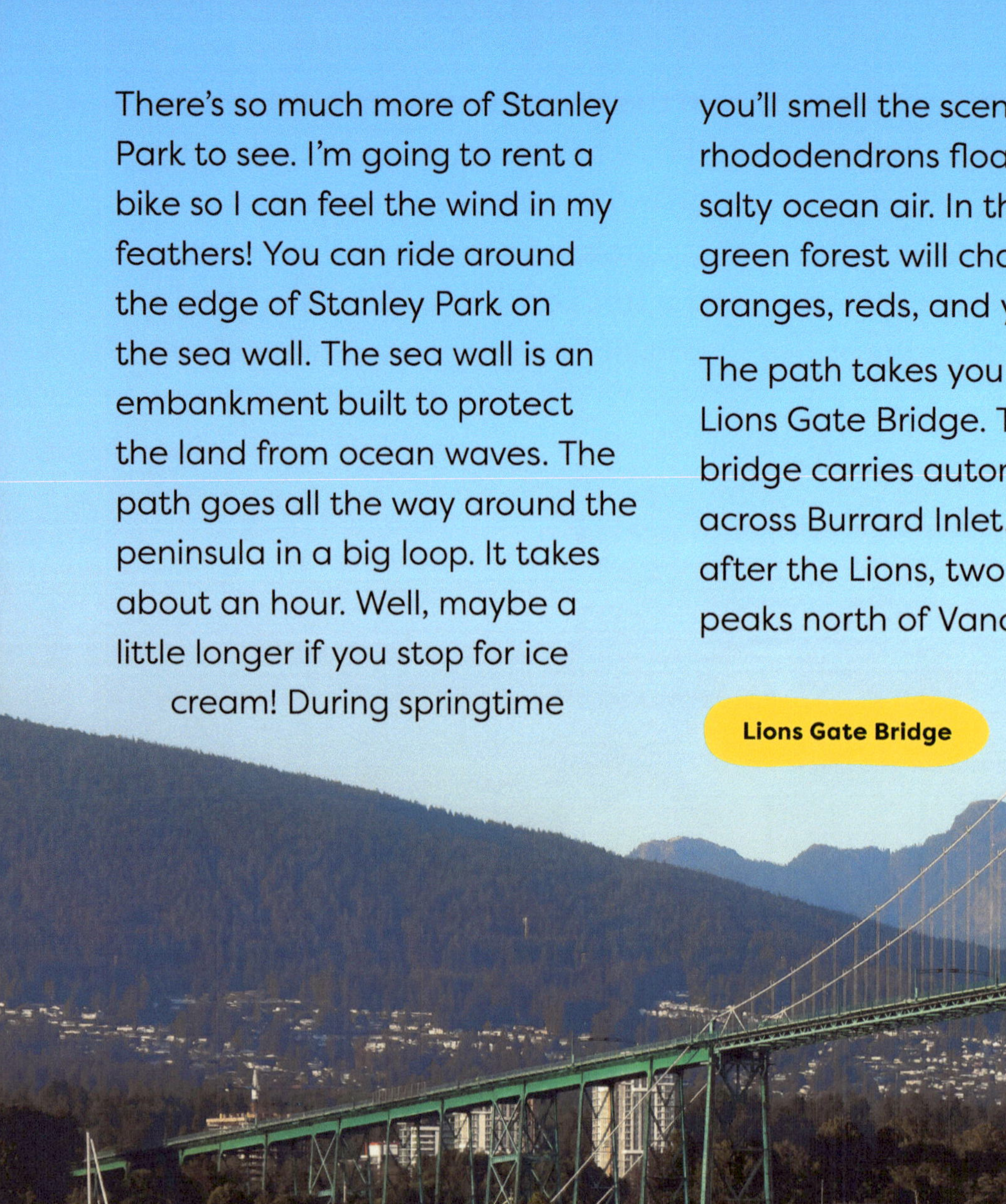

Lions Gate Bridge

The sea wall around Stanley Park is part of a longer waterfront path throughout Vancouver. At 17 miles (28 kilometers) long, it's the world's longest waterfront pathway!

Keep an eye out for seals, which like to pop their heads up along the coastline or nap on a rock. You'll find beaches where you can nap or swim, too. Farther offshore, look for big ships from around the world. They are waiting their turn to load or unload cargo.

Look out for more totem poles in Stanley Park!

Beaches

On sunny summer days, it gets warm in the city. Luckily for the people who live here and visitors like me, Vancouver has nine beaches! The weather here is cool in summer and mild in winter. This is because Vancouver has a humid oceanic climate. The ocean currents help keep the air over the land warmer in winter and cooler in summer. Because of this, it hardly ever gets cold enough to snow here, even though we are far north.

Kitsilano Beach, English Bay Beach, and the beaches in Stanley Park are fun and popular places to spend the day. You can go kayaking, play beach volleyball, or just paddle in the waves!

You might spot giant driftwood logs on many of Vancouver's beaches. The logs were once tall trees in a nearby forest. After they were cut down, they traveled on a logging truck and were unloaded into the ocean. There, they were tied together and a tugboat pulled them to a mill, a factory for turning logs into lumber or paper. These driftwood logs must have broken loose. What a journey!

Vanier Park

Wow! Have you ever seen such a massive crab?

This stainless steel crab with raised pincers stands in front of the H. R. MacMillan Space Centre in Vanier Park. It is 20 feet (6 meters) tall! It makes me think of a First Nations' legend about a crab that protected the harbor.

Inside the space center, you can explore space in the Planetarium, or touch a moon rock. Don't forget to take a selfie in the astronaut suit! Can you picture a puffin as Canada's next astronaut?

The crab sculpture was designed by the Canadian sculptor George Norris.

Maybe this will be my prize-winning photo! If you're in the mood for more museums, Vanier Park is also home to the Museum of Vancouver and the Vancouver Maritime Museum. I think you could spend the whole day here exploring different museums!

This isn't the only crab in Vanier Park, although it is definitely the biggest one! Flip over a rock at Vanier Park's beach and you might be startled! Often, a little green shore crab will skitter out sideways, running for cover.

Queen Elizabeth Park

The beautiful Queen Elizabeth Park is the highest point in Vancouver!

In addition to exploring the park filled with plants, trees, and flowers, you can also enjoy incredible views of the city. In spring and summer, artists come to Painters' Corner in the park to create and sell their artwork. I bet the artists are inspired by the park and its plants. I am for sure – I've taken so many photos here!

For a total change of scenery, head to the unusual dome inside the park. It's called the Bloedel Conservatory, and it is a paradise of tropical plants and flowers. It's a great place to warm up on a wet day.

"Squawk!" "Wheeeet!" "Dee-dee-dee!" Hey, it's loud in the conservatory! Over 100 brightly colored birds live here and fly around wherever they want. I see some bird friends from my travels around the world, including parrots, finches, and cockatoos. There are three habitats beneath the dome: tropical rain forest, subtropical rain forest, and desert. These habitats are fun to visit, but I think they'd be too hot for me to live in full time. I'm used to the chilly north!

Granville Island

Granville is Granville Island! This island used to be a mud flat that disappeared at high tide.

In the early 1900's, the government decided to dredge (scoop out) this area and use those scoops to build up the land. Then mining and forestry companies built the warehouses and factories that are now used for stores and artist studios. You can watch artists at work making items for sale. It's a good place to buy souvenirs!

You can get to Granville Island by ferry, water taxi, or by road.

Granville Island Public Market is a popular destination for Vancouverites when they need fresh fruit and veggies or seafood. This place is filled with colors, smells, and exciting food to try. You can look at the shiny salmon piled up on scoops of ice, and watch the crabs poking around in big tanks.

There are food booths everywhere with snacks to buy. Candied salmon, blueberries, goat cheese, brownies ... almost everything is made, grown, or caught nearby. Yum! Which of these snacks would you like to try?

Science World

Wait ... that's not a golf ball! That's Science World, my next stop.

Locals call Science World "the golf ball," but it's actually a geodesic dome, a dome built with flat triangles that fit together. This type of structure is super-strong because of the way the triangles naturally push against one another.

Inside Science World, you can run on the giant hamster wheel and shoot water to find out about capturing energy. It's fun learning about sustainability. We can make everyday lifestyle choices that help to protect nature, like taking public transport instead of a car.

Can you guess how many triangles there are on the outside of Science World? Try counting them! (There are 766 in all!)

There's something very unusual in the outdoor science park – chickens in the middle of the city! Raising chickens for eggs is another sustainable choice, and we can learn how here. Some Vancouverites have backyard chicken coops.

Before I go, I want to crawl through the beaver lodge. Did you know the beaver is a national symbol of Canada and appears on the five-cent coin? Beaver pelts were valuable when Indigenous people traded with the Europeans in the 1600's.

Chinatown

If you're looking for beautiful gates and peaceful gardens, head to Chinatown!

It's just a short ride from Science World on the SkyTrain. The train runs on a track above the streets. It's fun to see the city from up here! Vancouver has one of the largest Chinatowns in North America. Why? Thousands of Chinese people immigrated to Vancouver in the late 1800's to help build railroads. Many of their descendants are still here.

You'll know you're in Chinatown when you spot the Millennium Gate and the pagoda roofs, which curve up on the edges. There's so much to do here: visit the markets, do a tea tasting, and eat dim sum – little buns and dumplings served in bamboo steamers. They're delivered on small carts that are pushed around the restaurant.

Speaking of traditions, you'll find some very old gardening traditions at the Dr. Sun Yat-Sen Classical Chinese Garden. The traditions began when the Ming family ruled China, from the 1300's to the 1600's. They thought that we should pay attention to the rocks, water, and buildings, not just the plants. Everything should fit together.

The garden is influenced by yin and yang, opposites that create balance – for example heavy, jagged rocks next to smooth, still water.

Gastown

The Gastown neighborhood next to Chinatown is where the city first took root in the late 1800's.

The Gastown Steam Clock is powered by steam! It lets off steam each hour and toots a little tune every 15 minutes. It sounds a bit like a train whistle!

You might have seen the Flatiron Building in New York City (U.S.A.), but did you know that Vancouver has a flatiron building as well?! This narrow building in Gastown was built in the early 1900's and was once a hotel.

Here there used to be a statue of a man known as "Gassy" Jack Deighton. He was called "gassy" because of his long and crazy stories that must've seemed like a lot of hot air. Jack arrived here in 1867 and started building up what is now Vancouver.

Jack didn't have much money, but he had whiskey, a kind of alcohol that some grown-ups drink. So he talked some sawmill workers into building his bar in exchange for whiskey.

Jack's saloon was the first of many buildings in Gastown built with wood from nearby forests. Wood catches on fire easily, and the Great Fire of 1886 destroyed most of the city's original buildings. Many of the brick and stone buildings we see now with restaurants and stores were built just after the fire.

Vancouver Art Gallery

Before it was an art museum, this building used to be a courthouse.

Where better to find inspiration for my photos than at an art gallery ...

Vancouver Art Gallery to be precise! This gallery holds one of the largest collections of the paintings of the famous Canadian painter, Emily Carr. Have you ever heard of her before?

Emily Carr loved to draw when she was a little girl growing up on Vancouver Island in the late 1800's. She also loved to travel. She visited many First Nations villages in British Columbia. Look at her oil paintings. You can tell she was fascinated by two things: Indigenous culture and the beautiful, green landscape of British Columbia.

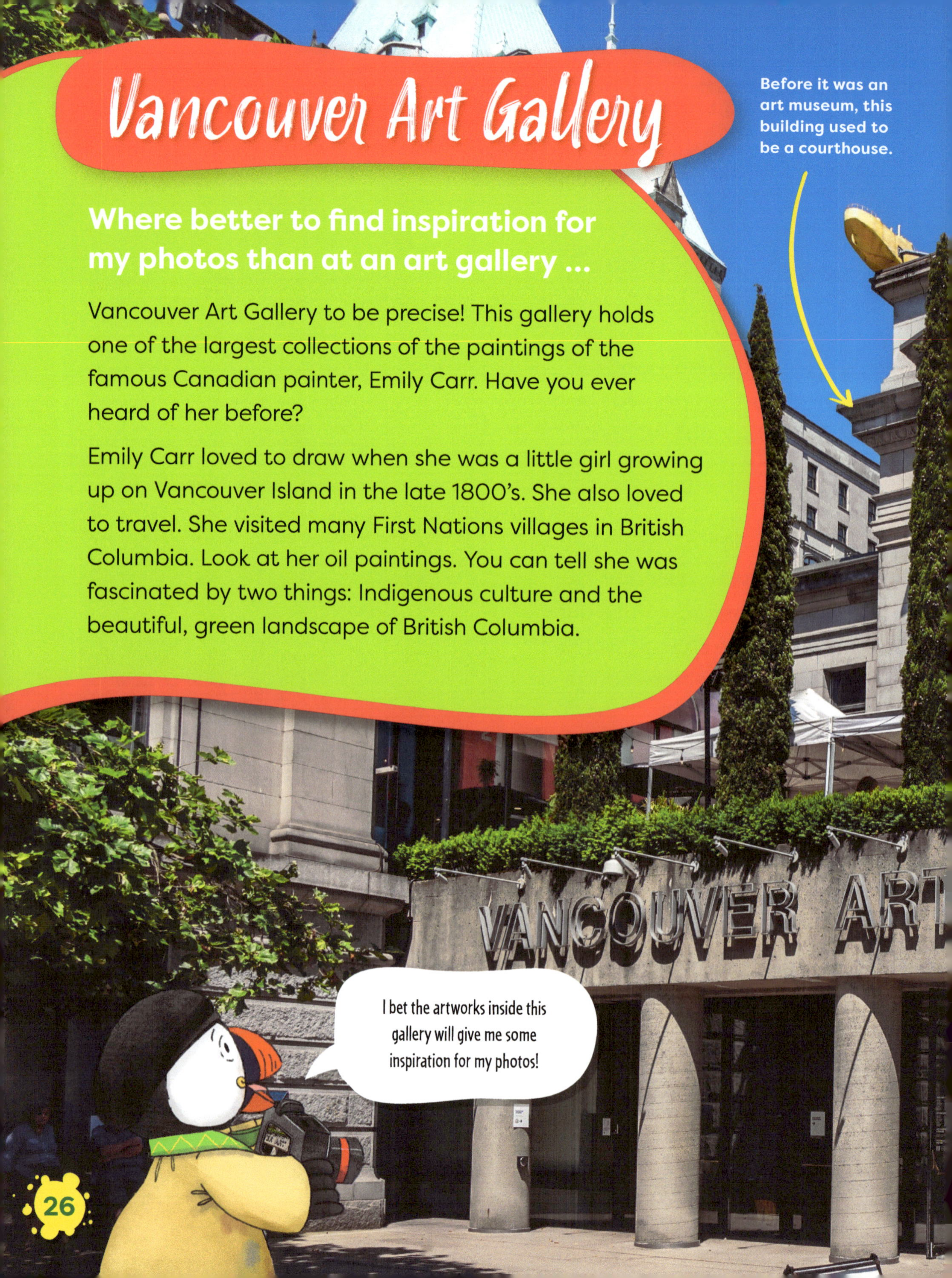

There are also many pieces by other Canadian artists here, including First Nations artworks, as well as art from around the world. In total, there are over 12,000 artworks! I think I might need to come back another day!

This Emily Carr painting shows First Nations totem poles.

There's so much outdoor art in Vancouver, like this digital orca. Other outdoor statues include a 65-foot (20-meter) water droplet, a poodle on a pole, and 14 giant laughing men, made of bronze.

Hockey

When many people think of hockey, they think of Canada.

Ice hockey is a contact sport and injuries are common, so players wear a helmet, gloves, pads, and a mouth guard to protect themselves.

It's more than just a sport here. It's part of the national identity. The National Hockey League (NHL) started in Canada. And what was once printed on the $5 bill? A drawing of kids playing hockey on a pond!

The logo of the Vancouver Canucks is an orca (killer whale) drawn in the style of the Haida First Nations people. The orca forms the shape of a letter "C."

Lots of Canadian kids learn to play when they are quite young on frozen ponds and backyard rinks. Some wake up when it's still dark, go to practices before school, and dream of becoming NHL players!

Vancouver cheers wildly for its hometown hockey team, the Vancouver Canucks. Canuck is another word for a Canadian person. That's like calling them the Vancouver Canadians! The Canucks play at Rogers Arena. If you visit during their season (from October to early April), maybe you can catch a game. The stadium is also used for other sports events and concerts.

Some of Canada's proudest hockey moments happened in 2010 during the Winter Olympics in Vancouver. The men's team played the United States for the gold medal and won in overtime. The Canadian women's team beat the U.S. team to win the gold medal, too!

Vancouver Lookout

Welcome to the Vancouver Lookout!

I've seen Vancouver from the ground looking up. Now it's time to see it from the sky looking down! Inside the Vancouver Lookout, you can take a high-speed glass elevator and zoom up to the observation deck 553 feet (169 meters) in the sky. That's as high as 30 giraffes standing on top of another!

This deck is a cool place to see the mountains, the ocean, and the clouds. If you're here at the right time, you can watch float planes landing or taking off for distant islands and remote fishing lodges. You might also spot cruise ships headed for Alaska.

You can spot many Vancouver landmarks from the observation deck, including Stanley Park and downtown skyscrapers.

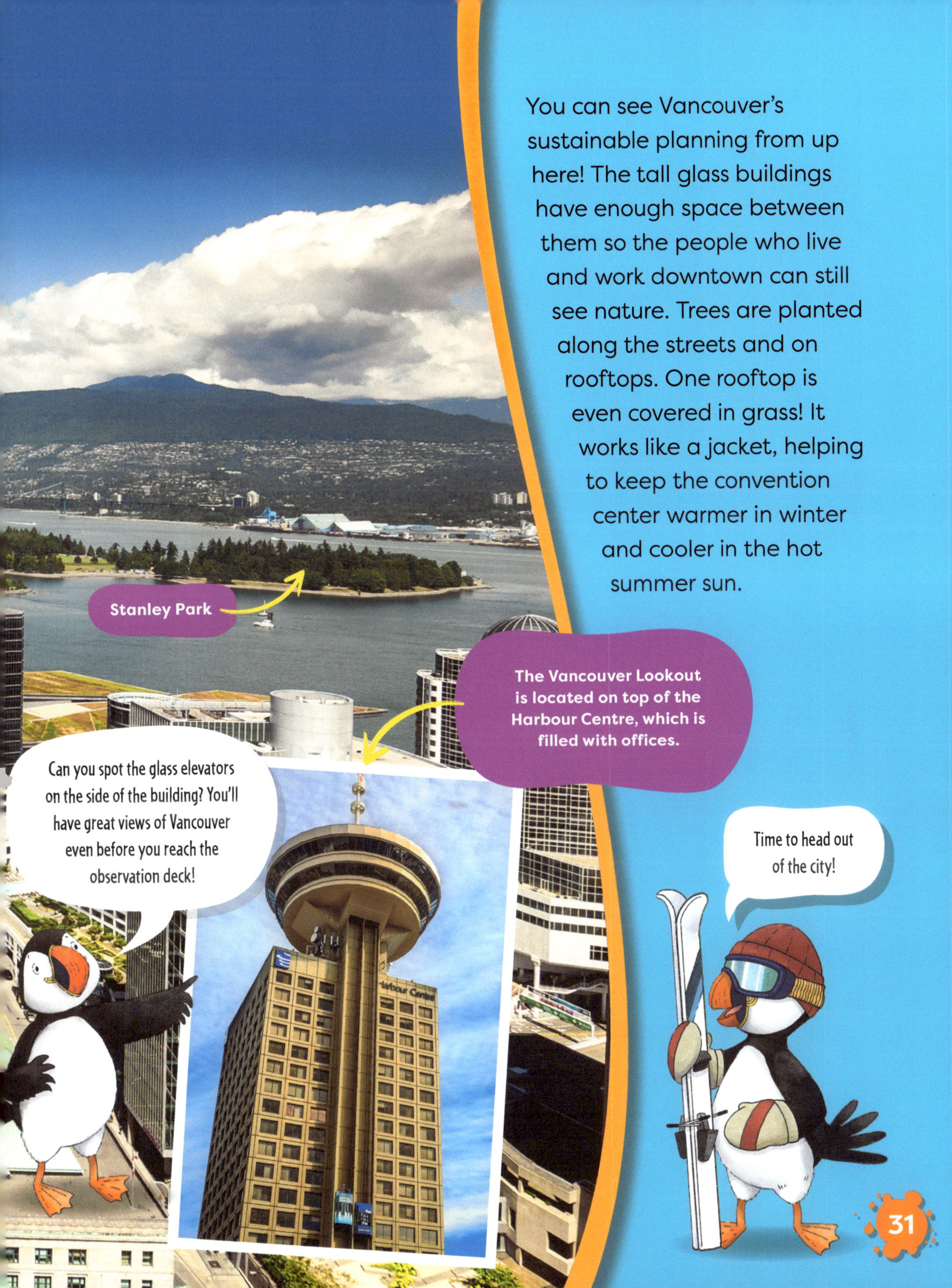

You can see Vancouver's sustainable planning from up here! The tall glass buildings have enough space between them so the people who live and work downtown can still see nature. Trees are planted along the streets and on rooftops. One rooftop is even covered in grass! It works like a jacket, helping to keep the convention center warmer in winter and cooler in the hot summer sun.

Grouse Mountain

You don't have to travel too far out of Vancouver to ski.

Grouse Mountain is less than 18 miles (30 kilometers) away on Vancouver's North Shore. To get to the top, climb aboard the gondola (a car that hangs from a cable). On the way up, look for Vancouver Island and the nearby Cascade mountains.

In winter, people come to Grouse Mountain to ski and snowboard. Popular summer activities include hiking and zip lining – riding on a long cable that you can strap onto and whoosh down the mountainside. That sounds like fun!

My favorite, though, is seeing rescued bears at the grizzly refuge. They love exploring their large enclosure and taking a dip in the ponds. There aren't any wild grizzlies on the North Shore, but black bears live here. Keep an eye out for sooty grouse as well. The first hikers to reach the peak of the mountain in 1894 named it Grouse Mountain after the bird, as they'd seen so many of them on their way up!

Can you spot Vancouver over there in the distance?

The name "grizzly bear" comes from the bears' coarse white- or silver-tipped outer hairs, which give them a grizzled (grayish) appearance.
The Skyride gondola is the perfect way to travel to the top of Grouse Mountain.
These photos are going to be epic!
More mountains

Mount Seymour

Mount Seymour is another peak in the North Shore Mountains, about 16 miles (25 kilometers) north of downtown Vancouver.

The mountain and the park around it are home to ancient forests of western hemlock, cedar, and Douglas fir trees. You can hike, mountain bike, or ride horses through forest trails around the base of the mountain. As you climb higher, the forest ends and there are meadows filled with flowers that bloom in spring and summer. If you're quiet and lucky, you might spot such wildlife as deer, coyotes, or even a cougar!

At the top of the mountain, there are ski, snowboard, and toboggan routes for use during the snowy winter. It's too snowy to hike up here in the winter, unless you're wearing snowshoes. Wearing snowshoes is a bit like hiking with a pair of tennis rackets strapped to your boots! The shoes spread out your weight so you don't sink into the snow. Indigenous people used to make them with animal skins stretched across a frame. Have you ever tried snowshoeing before?

Capilano Suspension Bridge

This isn't the place for you if you are scared of heights!

The first Capilano Suspension Bridge was made from woven ropes. Today, the bridge is supported by strong cables that could hold the weight of a jumbo jet airplane and all of its passengers!

The Cliffwalk path may look narrow and thin, but don't worry! It can support the weight of 35 adult orcas!

The Capilano Suspension Bridge hangs among the trees and above the Capilano River without any towers to support it. Each end is anchored, but there is nothing else in between that holds it up. Do you remember seeing the Lions Gate suspension bridge earlier? That bridge is a little different. Its cables transfer the weight to towers that support most of the load.

The water in the Capilano River comes from melting snow and rain high in the North Coast Mountains. The water rushes downhill in streams and rivers, like the Capilano. The rivers then empty into the ocean. What an adventure!

After the bridge, head to the Cliffwalk path. This pathway grips the steep canyon wall. Treetops Adventure is up next – seven smaller bridges rising into the evergreens. My heart is racing! Back on the ground, you can hike rain forest trails and explore the First Nations center.

Salmon

The Capilano River is one of many rivers around Vancouver where big salmon swim and leap upstream.

They are working hard to get to the place where they spawn (lay eggs). After they hatch, salmon spend a year or more in the river before swimming out to sea. Some kinds of salmon live in the ocean for 1 year, but others live there for 8 years. Somehow, their bodies know when it's time to return to the same exact river where they hatched. They fight their way upstream, or "run," in summer and fall.

Bears gather by rivers during the salmon run and catch as much fish as possible!

By this time, the males' bodies have really changed, with bright colors and hooked jaws. The females spawn in the gravel riverbed, the males fertilize the eggs, then all the grown-ups die.

In some places, overfishing, pollution, and loss of habitat have affected salmon populations. To help the salmon population recover, baby salmon are raised in hatcheries. A hatchery is a large tank with thousands of baby salmon inside. In the spring, the hatchery releases salmon ready to make their journey to the ocean.

Steveston Village

I was just on the north side of Vancouver. Now it's time to explore the south side in a historic village called Steveston.

The village sits at the mouth of the Fraser River (where it flows into the ocean). Follow the smell of saltwater – and the seagull noise – to the Steveston docks. You can walk past commercial fishing boats and peek inside to see the salmon, prawns (large shrimp), halibut, and cod caught today!

If you'd rather cook your own meal, why not buy some freshly caught fish off one of the many fishing boats in Steveston docks. How do you like to eat fish?

In the late 1800's, Steveston was the West Coast's largest fishing port. More than 15 canneries lined the waterfront. A cannery is a place where fish and other seafood are cut into pieces and packed into containers ... a very slimy business!

One of those canneries, the Gulf of Georgia Cannery, is now a museum. Go in and look at the long lines of cans. Can you imagine working there, surrounded by steam, clattering machines, and stinky fish? You can try out a cannery worker's tool known as a peugh (pew), a sharp spear used to move slippery fish.

Fort Langley National Historic Site

I've only gone about 30 miles (50 kilometers) east of Vancouver, but here at the Fort Langley National Historic Site, it feels like I've traveled two hundred years back in time!

Do you know what a cooperage is? Can you guess from the photo?! Here, craftspeople made barrels to transport traded items.

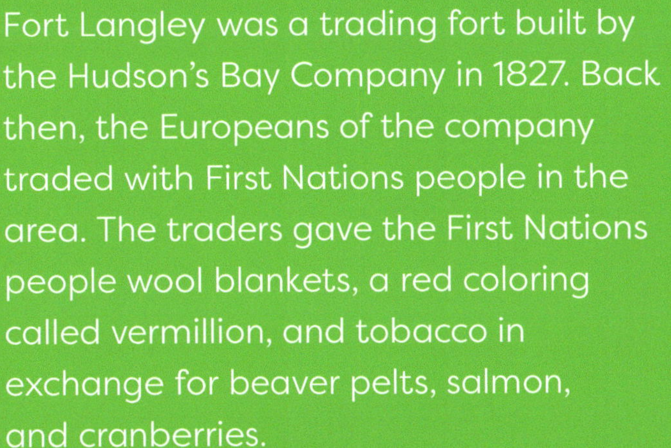

Fort Langley was a trading fort built by the Hudson's Bay Company in 1827. Back then, the Europeans of the company traded with First Nations people in the area. The traders gave the First Nations people wool blankets, a red coloring called vermillion, and tobacco in exchange for beaver pelts, salmon, and cranberries.

The Hudson's Bay Company traders sent beaver pelts (skin with the fur left on) to England, where they were turned into felt hats. The Indigenous people received wool blankets, which they made into coats. You can buy a similar blanket today at "Hudson's Bay" department store - the same Hudson's Bay Company that set up trading posts nearly 200 years ago!

In the blacksmith's store, you can see the red hot metal as it is hammered and shaped into tools. The people who work here are dressed like they're from the 1800's.

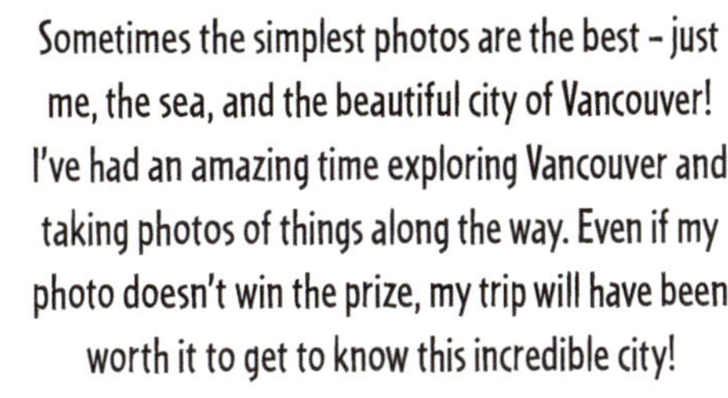

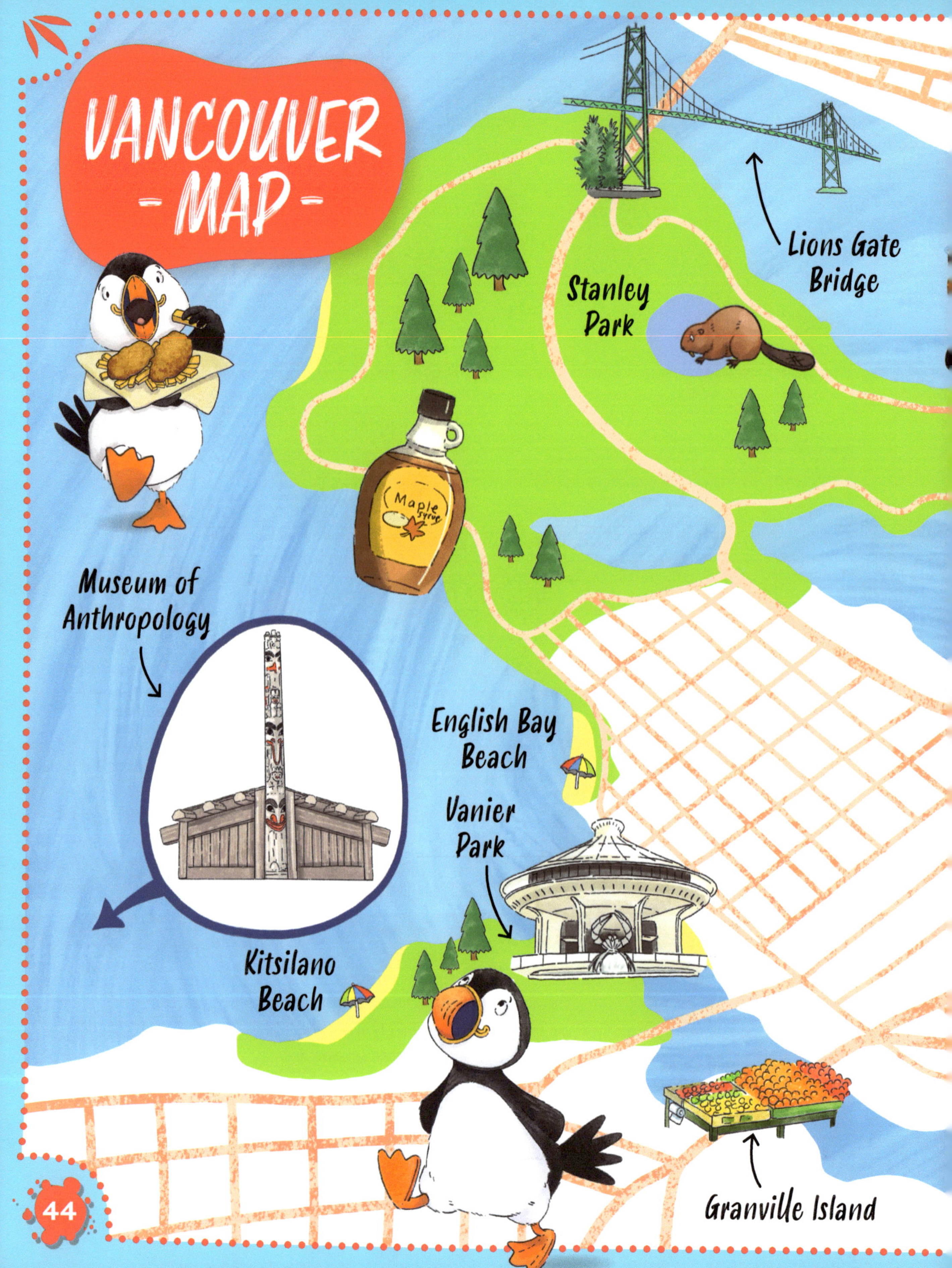
VANCOUVER
- MAP -
Lions Gate
Bridge
Stanley
Park
Maple
Syrup
Museum of
Anthropology
English Bay
Beach
Vanier
Park
Kitsilano
Beach
Granville Island

Vancouver Lookout
Vancouver Art Gallery
Harbour Centre
Gastown
VANCOUVER ART GALLERY
Chinatown
Rogers Arena
Queen Elizabeth Park
Science World

A Day in Vancouver

Be on the lookout for totem poles, dugout canoes, sculptures, and other art from First Nations people.

Start your day at the Museum of Anthropology to learn about the history of Vancouver!

Did you remember your swimsuit?

Make your way to Kitsilano Beach to enjoy some of Vancouver's natural beauty. Swim in the English Bay or take a dip in the seawater pool!

Time to travel! Hop on one of Vancouver's aquabus ferries and make your way over to Granville Island.

Keep your eyes on the water; you may spot a whale!

Granville Island is the perfect spot for a meal. From fresh fruits and veggies to seafood and even goat cheese, you're sure to enjoy the local fare.

Head back to the mainland and over to Rogers Arena for a Vancouver Canucks game. Cheer as the team skates across the rink – GOALLL!

Brr! It's a little chilly in here. Did you bring your jacket?

Where Am I?

Destination 1

This historic village is located on the south side of Vancouver.

You're sure to smell this destination as you get closer and closer!

Tour the Gulf of Georgia Cannery Museum to learn all about the slimy fish business!

Destination 2

Visitors can learn all about sustainability through fun, interactive exhibits.

Staff members raise chickens for eggs right in the middle of the city!

This destination's nickname is "the golf ball" because of its geodesic dome.

Destination 3

You'll need to ride a gondola to reach the top of this destination.

Visitors can ski and snowboard in the winter or hike and zip line in the summer!

While visiting, be on the lookout for such wildlife as black bears and grouse.

Destination 4

In the past, this building was a courthouse.

Today, this destination holds the largest collection of work by Canadian painter Emily Carr.

Check out other Canadian artwork, including aboriginal pieces from the past as well as today.

Destination 5

Visiting this destination feels like traveling back in time 200 years!

Watch blacksmiths, coopers, and other tradespeople work.

Learn about how the Hudson Bay Company traded with the First Nations people.

Destination 6

Test your fear of heights crossing this destination as it sways in the treetops.

Visitors can also check out the Treetops Adventure or Cliffwalk path.

This destination is located high above the Capilano River.

Answers on page 55

Photos from Vancouver

Treetop Adventure

Stanley Park

Mount Seymour

Vancouver Lookout and Gastown

Bloedel Conservatory

Lions Gate Bridge

H. R. MacMillan Space Centre

Engage Your Reader

Activate background knowledge, set the purpose for reading, and monitor comprehension with this tried-and-true reading strategy!

Work with your reader(s) to create a KWL chart. Take some time to discuss what students already KNOW about Vancouver as well as what they WONDER about the city. You will revisit what they LEARNED after reading the book.

KNOW	WONDER	LEARNED

1. Have readers preview the structure of this text by flipping through the pages. Page 5 describes how clues are included for Norrie the puffin's next destinations.
2. Set the tone for reading: *As you read, think about all the different places in Vancouver and how history, culture, and people have shaped them into what they are today.*
3. After reading each section, revisit the KWL chart. Brainstorm what readers LEARNED from this section and add it to the chart. Your reader can add other wonderings they may have had, too!

Consider these questions to guide the brainstorming process:

- Why is location important to places, history, and culture?
- What patterns do you notice in the placement of things around the city of Vancouver?
- What makes Vancouver unique?

Use these comprehension questions to help your reader(s) check their understanding as they navigate the text.

p. 6-7 Who first lived on Vancouver's land thousands of years ago?

What do totems represent?

p. 8-9 Why might the First Nations people have built their villages on the Stanley Park peninsula?

p. 10-11 Describe the nature and wildlife of Stanley Park.

p. 12-13 Why are the beaches in Vancouver cool in the summer and mild in the winter?

p. 14-15 What would you enjoy most about a visit to Vanier Park?

p. 16-17 What three habitats are featured at the Bloedel Conservatory at Queen Elizabeth Park?

p. 18-19 How did Granville Island come to be?

p. 20-21 What is sustainability and how can you learn about it at Science World?

p. 22-23 When and why did many Chinese people originally immigrate to Vancouver?

p. 24-25 Why are most buildings in Gastown made of brick and stone if this neighborhood was originally constructed of wood?

p. 26-27 Who was Emily Carr and why is she important to Vancouver and Canada?

p. 28-29 What is hockey? What does it mean to the city of Vancouver?

p. 30-31 You can see unique views from the Vancouver Lookout. Of all the sights described, what would you be most interested in viewing?

p. 32-33 How did Grouse Mountain get its name?

What do people enjoy doing at Grouse Mountain?

p. 34-35 What are snowshoes and how do they work?

p. 36-37 Would you cross the Capilano Suspension Bridge? What about the Cliffwalk path or Treetops Adventure? Why or why not?

p. 38-39 What does it mean when salmon "run" in the summer and fall?

p. 40-41 What are you likely to find at Steveston Village?

p. 42-43 Today, Fort Langley is a National Historic Site. What was it like when it originally opened in 1827?

Extend Through Writing

Norrie the puffin just took you on a tour of Vancouver, Canada! Based on the places highlighted in this book, where would you like to visit in Vancouver?

Your written response should include:

- An introduction, including a general statement about Vancouver
- At least three places you would like to visit and at least three reasons why these places interest you
- A conclusion in which you briefly restate your interest in these three famous Vancouver destinations

Copy this graphic organizer onto another sheet of paper or visit **www.worldbook.com/resources** to download and print a copy. Use it to help you plan your writing.

Introduction:		
Destination 1	Destination 2	Destination 3
Reason 1	Reason 1	Reason 1
Reason 2	Reason 2	Reason 2
Reason 3	Reason 3	Reason 3
Conclusion:		

Answers

Where Am I? answers, p. 48-49:

1. Steveston Village, 2. Science World, 3. Grouse Mountain, 4. Vancouver Art Gallery, 5. Fort Langley National Historic Site, 6. Capilano Suspension Bridge

Comprehension question answers, p. 53:

p. 6-7

The First Nations people lived on Vancouver's land thousands of years ago. They created totem poles with carvings of different creatures that represented special meanings and told the story of their families.

p. 8-9

The First Nations people may have built their villages on Stanley Park peninsula because it was a great location for fishing as well as gathering other natural resources, like tall cedar trees.

p. 10-11

Visitors of Stanley Park can enjoy the ocean waves, roses, rhododendrons, and beautiful fall foliage. Be on the lookout for seals and other wildlife!

p. 12-13

The beaches in Vancouver are cool in the summer and mild in the winter because the ocean currents affect the temperature of the air. Vancouver has a humid oceanic climate.

p. 14-15

Answers may vary.

p. 16-17

The Bloedel Conservatory at Queen Elizabeth Park includes a tropical rain forest habitat, a subtropical rain forest habitat, and a desert habitat.

p. 18-19

In the past, Granville Island was a mud flat that disappeared at high tide. In the early 1900's, the government dredged the land and then used it to build up the island.

p. 20-21

Sustainability is all about making choices that help protect nature and our planet. At Science World, you can learn about capturing energy in different forms and even about sustainable eating.

p. 22-23

Many Chinese people immigrated to Vancouver in the late 1800's for work. They helped build Vancouver's railroads.

p. 24-25

Although Gastown originally boasted wooden buildings, the Great Fire of 1886 burned most of the city. New brick and stone buildings were constructed shortly after.

p. 26-27

Emily Carr grew up on Vancouver Island during the late 1800's. She traveled, visiting many First Nations villages and creating artwork. She loved the beauty of nature and aboriginal culture. You can see much of her artwork at the Vancouver Art Gallery.

p. 28-29

Hockey is a contact sport where a team of athletes skate on an ice rink attempting to shoot a puck into a goal. Hockey is a part of Canada's national identity, and Vancouver is home to a famous NHL team, the Canucks!

p. 30-31

Answers may vary.

p. 32-33

Grouse Mountain is so named for the birds - grouse - that live there.

People visit Grouse Mountain to ski, snowboard, hike, go zip lining, or visit the bears at the grizzly refuge.

p. 34-35

Snowshoes are almost like tennis rackets that strap to user's feet. The wide platforms allow users to step on top of the snow without sinking into it because the shoes help spread out their weight.

p. 36-37

Answers may vary.

p. 38-39

Salmon "run" in the summer and fall. This means they fight their way upstream, swimming hard (and sometimes even jumping out of the water!) to travel back to the exact river where they hatched. Once there, they spawn (lay eggs).

p. 40-41

Steveston Village is known for fishing. The village is located at the mouth of Fraser River. Many canneries and fish stands are located at the Steveston Docks.

p. 42-43

When Fort Langley originally opened in 1827, it was home to the Hudson's Bay Company. The company was known for trading with the First Nations people.

Glossary

Aboriginal *(ab uh RIHJ uh nuhl)* **peoples of Australia** The first people to live on the continent of Australia and their descendants. *Aboriginal* comes from the Latin words *ab origine*, which mean *from the beginning.*

colony *(KOL uh nee)* A settlement set up by people outside their native land, and ruled by the settlers' home country

convict *(KON vihkt)* A person who has been found guilty of a crime

ferry *(FEHR ee)* A boat used to carry people, vehicles, or cargo across narrow bodies of water

habitat *(HAB uh tat)* The kind of place in which a living thing usually lives

Vancouverite *(SIHD nee seye duhr)* A person who lives in Vancouver

Index

www.ingramcontent.com/pod-product-compliance
Ingram Content Group UK Ltd.
Pitfield, Milton Keynes, MK11 3LW, UK
UKHW060106300726
14090UKWH00003B/381

* 9 7 8 0 7 1 6 6 5 3 3 3 2 *